Always Be ΓΙΜΟ!! ☺

Jim

the
sad
mad
glad
book

The Anatomy of Your Attitude

Chuck Stump & Jim Strawn

Put your Best Foot Forward!

Chuck Stump

The Sad Mad Glad Book-The Anatomy of Your Attitude

For permissions, to order additional copies of this title, or to contact the authors, call or write:

Four Dolphins Press, LLC
P. O. Box 833, Scott Depot, West Virginia, 25560
Phone (304) 757-8125
Visit our Web site at www.fourdolphins.net

Printed in the United States of America
First Edition: October 2007
Second Printing: April 2008

ISBN: 978-0-9799315-1-2

Four Dolphins Press would like to give the following people a pat on the back for lending a helping hand.

<u>Graphic Design</u>
Michael Teel - Progressity, Inc., Charleston, WV
<u>Editors</u>
Nancy Wallace and Pat Hendricks
<u>Publishing Consultant</u>
Patrick Grace - Grace Associates, LLC, Huntington, WV
<u>JE Robins Elementary, Charleston, WV</u>
Grades 3,4 and 5, 2007
<u>West Teays Elementary, Hurricane, WV</u>
Grades 3,4 and 5, 2007

*Dedicated to Sarah Stump, and to Brendan and Rachel,
the two most special children in the world, who bring
Sad and Mad – but mostly Glad to my world.*

Look at your body.

You have ears and eyes, and arms and legs.

That's no surprise.

Your body can teach you about different moods, and about your many

attitudes.

Some animal friends will help us explain,

because some of our parts are exactly the same.

Your **attitude** is controlled with thoughts from your brain.

They get there as fast as a speeding train.

Think about your attitude.

Think quite a lot.

When you're glad
it's good.

When you're **mad**
it's **not**.

With some tips and training,
day or night,
positive thoughts can keep
your attitude right.

We'll link these thoughts to body parts
as we go from the top of your head
to the tip of your toe.

With so many choices, where should we begin?

Here's an idea!

Let's start with your

skin.

It is hard to hurt feelings when skin is

"**thick**."

But when skin is

“thin,”

feelings get hurt quick!

Skin might be dark or might be light,

the same from head to toe.

No shade is wrong. No shade is right.

That's the important thing to know.

Do you have a friend whose skin is different from yours?

20

head

You need to remember to

"use your head."

This means *think before you act*.

Do this and you'll make fewer mistakes.

That's a very important fact!

Winners hold their heads up **high**.

Some losers hang their heads and

cry.

We need to learn that win or lose,

it's an honor to play and compete.

Sportsmanship, and shaking hands,

is what makes the game complete.

eyes

Your eyes are known as

the windows to the soul.

They make it hard to keep a surprise.

When you're happy,
a friend can take one glance
and see the "smile" in your eyes.

When you're scared your eyes
get **big** and **wide**!

When you're sad, they say, "I hurt inside."
When was the last time you were
sad?

**What changed your attitude
and made you feel better?**

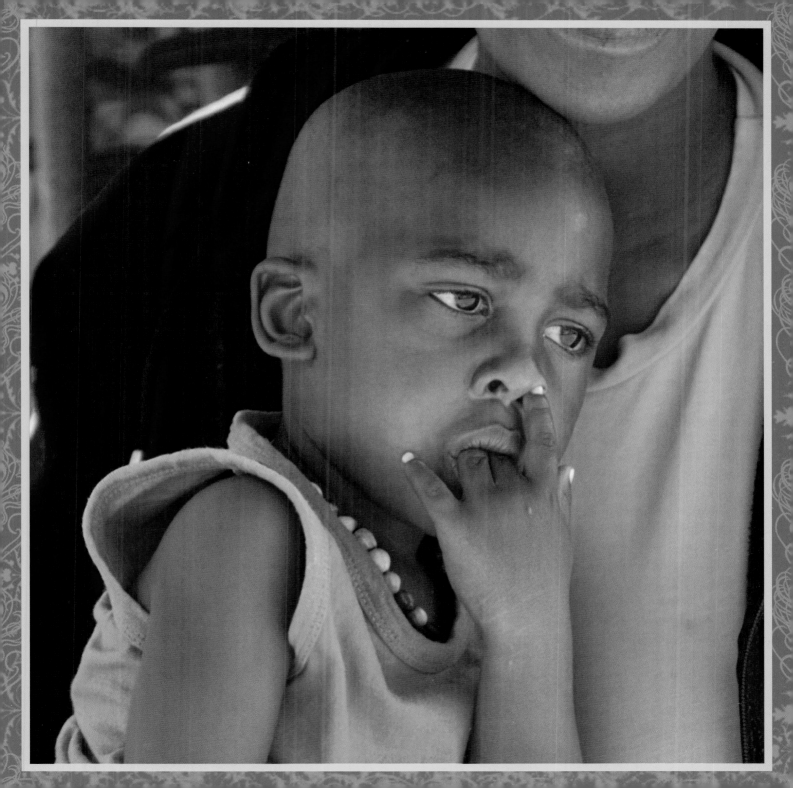

nose

Your nose is found in the center of your face.

It does a lot more than take up space.

If somebody reminds you to
"keep your nose clean,"
they're saying "**stay out of trouble**"
…if you know what I mean.

Rubbing noses is something you don't want to **miss**. For many people and cultures, it's the same as a **kiss**.

If you
"*stick your nose where it doesn't belong*",

you're being "nosey."

Have you heard that expression?

You need to know when to leave people alone.

This is another valuable lesson.

Perhaps the greatest thing we learn

from our noses, is to

take time to stop

and smell all the roses.

Slow down and be thankful for family and friends,

and enjoy the good times from beginning to end.

Below your nose, just an inch or two south,

is a magical thing. That's right – it's your

mouth.

It just does the work. Your brain is the boss.

Speak words that are true,

not words that are false.

What can happen if you don't tell the truth?

To have a large mouth is a wonderful thing

if your goal is to scream and shout.

But if you have a

"BIG mouth,"

you shouldn't be proud,

because your secrets will always leak out.

Do you have a hard time keeping secrets?

smile

A smile is a very special thing.

All people have their **own**.

The more you share yours with your friends,

The less you'll be **alone**!

Your

tongue

has taste buds for tasting food.

But

don't stick your tongue out

-- it's very rude.

When you think a thought that isn't nice,
it's best to **bite your tongue**.
This keeps the thought inside your head,
and damage from being done.

ears

If you use your ears to stop and listen,

you'll learn some things you might be missin'.

Whether you live in the north or the south, you have two **ears** but only one mouth. This teaches a lesson that it might be best, to listen more, and talk much less.

neck

Below your head you'll find your neck.

It's right above your shoulders.

Here's something else you'll need to know

as you grow a little older.

A turtle lives inside a shell.

It keeps him safe and sound.

He has to stick his **neck** out
if he wants to get around.

To stick your neck out
means to take a chance,
to do something new or to try to advance.

**When was the last time you
tried something new?**

hands

Your hand has five fingers to grip, grab, and hold.

Some
hands
are young,

and some
hands
are old.

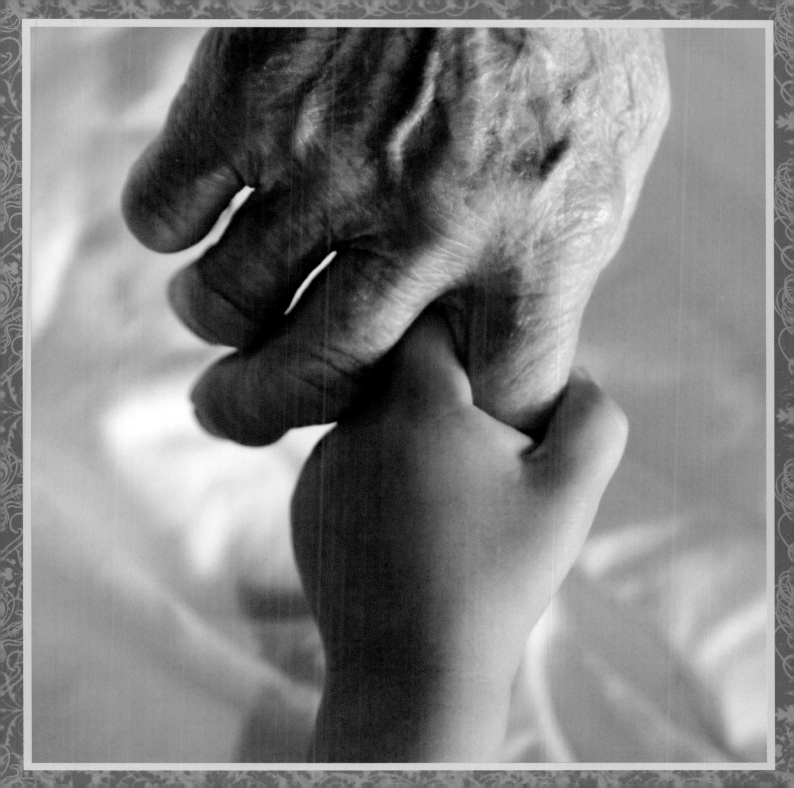

Your fingers and hands are special gifts.

They can be used to do work…

...or give someone a

To **lend a helping hand**

is a great lesson to learn.

It is important that we all work together.

When we all do our part,
even the heaviest load can feel
as light as a feather.

**Do you know someone who could
use a helping hand?**

Your **hands** can be used to show
people you care…

that no matter what happens,
you'll always be there.

A round of applause or a
pat on the back
says, "You're doing a great job!"
-- and keeps them on track.

**Do you know anyone who deserves
a *pat on the back?***

But, most of all,
hands should hold one another.

It could be your father or maybe your mother.

The gentle touch, and the warmth,
tells those who are near,

"You are safe with me. There is nothing to fear."

Whose hands do you like to hold?

back

When someone says, **"I've got your back,"**

they're protecting you from harm,

and if enemies get close to you,

they'll sound out the alarm.

Who's "got your back?"

lungs

When you get too excited, someone might say,

"Calm down. Breathe deep and slow."

Fresh air comes in and stress goes out.

It's that easy… now you know.

knees

Your knees should remind you to
get down and pray,

to be humble and thankful for the
gift of each day.

feet

Your feet work hard in dark smelly shoes,
carrying the load as we all move along.

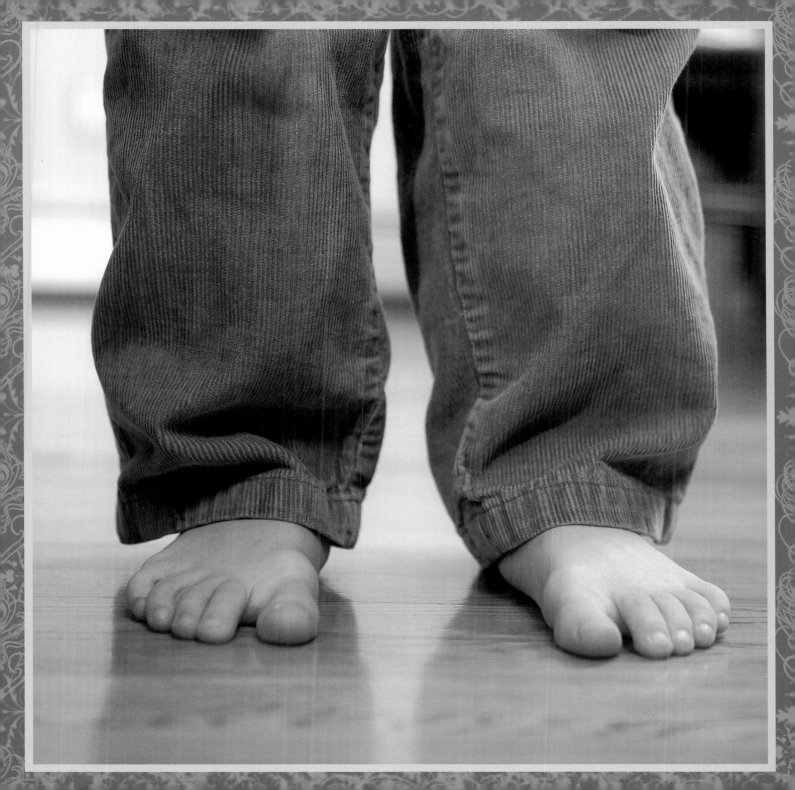

_____

But watch them bounce and tap and swing, when your ears hear your favorite song.

What is your favorite song?

_____

"Put your best foot forward"

is what most people say.

You should always do your very best.

Keep this thought in your head each day,

and you will finish well ahead of the rest.

heart

Skin and ears, mouths, hands and feet--
we've mentioned lots of parts.
But you just might learn the very most
by looking at your heart.

Whenever you don't get what you want
or something makes you sad,
you have what's called "**a broken heart**."
Sometimes, they hurt really bad.

Have you ever had a broken heart?

Then someone special comes along
to comfort and to care.

Your heart, once broken, now is fixed,
and **love** made the repair.

Some people say they're
"**young at heart.**"

They're always having fun.

They don't get tired or call it quits
until the day is done.

Generous people have
a heart of gold.

They're not selfish. They're not greedy.

They always want to help the poor,

unfortunate and needy.

**How do you show someone you
have a heart of gold?**

That's all for now, you've learned a **lot**,
and now you're really **smart**.
You've learned some lessons, big and small,
from different body parts.

Let each part be a reminder
to fill your life with good,
so those you meet will surely say…

"I like your **attitude!**"

The End

We would like to know what you think?
Go to www.fourdolphins.net and send
us your Book Report.

Thanks!

Chuck   *Jim*